Spelling Half Termly Tests

Year 6/P7

Clare Dowdall

William Collins' dream of knowledge for all began with the publication of his first book in 1819.
A self-educated mill worker, he not only enriched millions of lives, but also founded a flourishing
publishing house. Today, staying true to this spirit, Collins books are packed with inspiration,
innovation and practical expertise. They place you at the centre of a world of possibility
and give you exactly what you need to explore it.

Collins. Freedom to teach.

Collins
An imprint of HarperCollins*Publishers*
The News Building
1 London Bridge Street
London
SE1 9GF

Browse the complete Collins catalogue at **www.collins.co.uk**

© HarperCollins*Publishers* Limited 2018

10 9 8 7 6 5 4 3 2 1

ISBN 978-0-00-831155-1

All rights reserved. No part of this publication may be reproduced, stored in a retrieval system,
or transmitted in any form by any means, electronic, mechanical, photocopying, recording or otherwise,
without the prior written permission of the Publisher or a licence permitting restricted copying in
the United Kingdom issued by the Copyright Licensing Agency Ltd., Barnard's Inn, 86 Fetter Lane, London, EC4A 1EN.

British Library Cataloguing in Publication Data. A catalogue record for this publication is available from the British Library.

Author: Clare Dowdall
Publisher: Katie Sergeant
Senior Editor: Mike Appleton
Copyeditor: Tanya Solomons
Proofreader: Catherine Dakin
Cover designer: The Big Mountain Design, Ken Vail Graphic Design
Production controller: Katharine Willard

Contents

How to use this book	4

Year 6/P7 Word Lists

Autumn Half Term 1	6
Autumn Half Term 2	8
Spring Half Term 1	10
Spring Half Term 2	12
Summer Half Term 1	14
Summer Half Term 2	16

Year 6/P7 Half Termly Tests

Autumn Half Term 1 Test A	18
Autumn Half Term 1 Test B	22
Autumn Half Term 2 Test A	26
Autumn Half Term 2 Test B	30
Spring Half Term 1 Test A	34
Spring Half Term 1 Test B	38
Spring Half Term 2 Test A	42
Spring Half Term 2 Test B	46
Summer Half Term 1 Test A	50
Summer Half Term 1 Test B	54
Summer Half Term 2 Test A	58
Summer Half Term 2 Test B	62

Answers

Answers in Context	66
Word-only Answers	90
Year 6/P7 Spelling Record Sheet	92

How to use this book

Introduction

Collins Assessment Spelling Half Termly Tests have been designed to give you a consistent whole school approach to teaching and assessing spelling. Each photocopiable book covers the required rules, words and common exception words from the English National Curriculum statutory guidance and Spelling Appendix. For teachers in Scotland, the books can offer guidance and structure that is not provided in the Curriculum for Excellence Experiences and Outcomes or Benchmarks.

Revision of previous years' work is also included, where appropriate, to ensure children are building their skills to become confident and secure spellers. As standalone tests, independent of any teaching and learning scheme, *Collins Assessment Spelling Half Termly Tests* provide a structured way to assess progress in spelling, to identify areas for development, and to provide evidence towards expectations for each year group.

Why spelling matters

Spelling is a key focus of the 2014 English National Curriculum statutory requirements for writing, and the expectations and demands are significant. Out of a possible 70 marks, 20 are awarded for spelling in the Key Stage 2 National Tests, and 20 per cent of the new English Language GCSE 9–1 marks are allocated to spelling, punctuation and grammar. In Year 2, there is an optional Key Stage 1 English grammar, punctuation and spelling test that schools can use to help them make an assessment about children's spelling knowledge, as well as looking at their writing. In Scotland, the P1 literacy, P4 writing and P7 writing Scottish National Standardised Assessments assess spelling at early, first and second levels, respectively.

Focusing on spelling knowledge and skills will also benefit children's wider writing and will have a lasting impact across their education in primary, secondary and beyond. The *Collins Assessment Spelling Half Termly Tests* aim to support teachers to make assessments about children's confidence and use of required spelling rules and strategies, in order to support preparation for these standard assessment points.

How to use this book

The book is divided into two main sections. In the first section, between 30 and 36 weekly word lists are provided (depending on the year group). Each list contains six to ten words per half term. These words can be used for weekly tests and used in the classroom, or sent home with the children. They generally follow the order of the spelling rules as set out in the Spelling Appendix of the National Curriculum and include any words that are specified in the word lists and the non-statutory guidance.

In the second section, 12 half-termly tests are provided, offering two test options per half term: Test A and Test B. These tests offer an equivalent level of challenge and are designed to cover the spelling patterns for that half term's work. The spellings in the half-termly tests are presented in a random order within contextualised sentences. The sentences used are appropriate for the year group in terms of content, grammar and punctuation. The tests are designed to build experience and confidence with this format as well as to test children's spelling knowledge when writing in context.

Each test should take approximately 15 minutes. Guidance is provided for each test, with instructions to read out to the children and a script. The children write the word in the gap in the sentence on their test.

How to use this book

The tests have been written to ensure smooth progression in children's spelling ability within the book and across the rest of the books in series, enabling them to build on their spelling knowledge and show progress.

Marking the tests

The answers are provided in two formats for ease of use: in context and in short form for quick marking.

Recording progress

You can use the pupil-facing record sheets to provide evidence of the areas in which children have performed well and where they need to focus. A spreadsheet is provided in the downloadable version so results can easily be recorded for your classes, and any gaps in understanding can be identified. The spreadsheet can then be used to inform your next teaching and learning steps.

Editable download

All the files are available in Word and PDF format for you to edit if you wish. Go to collins.co.uk/assessment/downloads to find instructions on how to download. The files are password protected and the password clue is included on the website. You will need to use the clue to locate the password in your book.

Year 6/P7 Word lists – Autumn Half Term 1

Word list 1

accommodate
accompany
according
achieve
aggressive
accident
accidentally
actual
actually
address

Word list 2

available
average
awkward
bargain
bruise
breath
breathe
build
busy
business

Word list 3

competition
conscience
conscious
controversy
convenience
circle
complete
consider
continue
decide

Year 6/P7 Word lists – Autumn Half Term 1

Word list 4

determined
develop
dictionary
disastrous
embarrass
earth
eight
eighth
enough
exercise

Word list 5

excellent
existence
explanation
familiar
foreign
February
forward
fruit
grammar
group

Year 6/P7 Word lists – Autumn Half Term 2

Word list 6

amateur
ancient
apparent
appreciate
attached
answer
appear
arrive
believe
bicycle

Word list 7

category
cemetery
committee
communicate
community
calendar
caught
centre
century
certain

Word list 8

correspond
criticise
curiosity
definite
desperate
describe
different
difficult
disappear
early

Year 6/P7 Word lists – Autumn Half Term 2

Word list 9

environment
equipped
equipment
especially
exaggerate
experience
experiment
extreme
famous
favourite

Word list 10

forty
frequently
government
guarantee
harass
guard
guide
heard
heart
height

Year 6/P7 Word lists – Spring Half Term 1

Word list 1

hindrance
identity
immediate
immediately
individual
history
imagine
increase
important
interest

Word list 2

marvellous
mischievous
muscle
necessary
neighbour
material
medicine
mention
minute
natural

Word list 3

persuade
physical
prejudice
privilege
profession
opposite
ordinary
particular
peculiar
perhaps

Year 6/P7 Word lists – Spring Half Term 1

Word list 4

relevant
restaurant
rhyme
rhythm
sacrifice
potatoes
pressure
probably
promise
purpose

Word list 5

soldier
stomach
sufficient
suggest
symbol
remember
sentence
separate
special
straight

Year 6/P7 Word lists – Spring Half Term 2

Word list 6

interfere
interrupt
language
leisure
lightning
island
knowledge
learn
length
library

Word list 7

nuisance
occupy
occur
opportunity
parliament
naughty
notice
occasion
occasionally
often

Word list 8

programme
pronunciation
queue
recognise
recommend
popular
position
possess
possession
possible

Year 6/P7 Word lists – Spring Half Term 2

Word list 9

secretary
shoulder
signature
sincere
sincerely
quarter
question
recent
regular
reign

Word list 10

system
temperature
thorough
twelfth
variety
strange
strength
suppose
surprise
therefore

Year 6/P7 Word lists – Summer Half Term 1

Word list 1

vegetable
vehicle
yacht
though
although
thought
through
various
weight
vegetable

Word list 2

forgotten
beginning
regretted
preferred
gardening
obeyed
mystery
sympathy
touch
forgotten

Word list 3

disagree
dishonest
disappear
misheard
misfortune
incorrect
illegal
impossible
irresponsible
disagree

Year 6/P7 Word lists – Summer Half Term 1

Word list 4

reappear
rearrange
submerge
subtitle
superhuman
interact
international
antiseptic
autograph
reappear

Word list 5

information
sensation
happily
usually
originally
enclosure
measure
adventure
picture
information

Year 6/P7 Word lists – Summer Half Term 2

Word list 6

decision
television
vigorous
curious
rejection
election
hesitation
permission
possession
decision

Word list 7

chorus
echo
chef
brochure
plague
discipline
prey
neighbour
fascinate
chorus

Word list 8

gracious
anxious
artificial
essential
tolerance
decency
obedience
independence
hesitancy
gracious

Year 6/P7 Word lists – Summer Half Term 2

Word list 9

reliable
sensible
visibly
preference
transferring
receive
enough
brought
ceiling
reliable

Word list 10

island
doubt
accept
weather
alter
guessed
cereal
advise
morning
island

Year 6/P7 Autumn Half Term 1 Test A

Spelling rules and knowledge

- The words in this test can be used to check knowledge of the words from the statutory word lists for Years 3 to 6. Words from Years 3 and 4 are included for revision.

Guidance for teachers

The test is designed to build experience and confidence with this format, as well as to test children's spelling knowledge.
The test should take approximately 15 minutes.
Children should have a copy of the test and a pencil to use.
Children with specific needs should be given appropriate support.
All children should be encouraged to have a go at spelling each word, using the strategies that they have learnt.
Remind the children to check their answers by asking: *Does it look right? Does it sound right? Does it make sense in the sentence?*
Avoid over-emphasising the spelling of each word as you read it.

> Read each word aloud, saying: *The word is…*
> Next, read the sentence that includes the word.
> Wait for the children to attempt to write the word.
> Re-read the word, saying: *The word is…*

Remind the children to check the word before moving to the next spelling.
At the end of the test, read each sentence again and encourage the children to check back.

Instructions for children

(You may like to read this to the children prior to the test.)

This is a spelling test to check your knowledge of the spelling words we have worked on.
You need a pencil.
Please write your name, class and the date at the top of the test.
I will read a word out loud and then say it again in a sentence.
You should write the word in the gap in the sentence on your test.
I will read it again and give you time to check it.
Don't worry if you are not sure about a spelling. Have a go using the strategies we have learnt.
If you make a mistake, cross out the word and try again.

Words tested (20)

accommodate, available, competition, determined, excellent, achieve, bargain, controversy, disastrous, familiar, accidentally, breathe, complete, eight, forward, address, business, decide, exercise, group

Year 6/P7 Autumn Half Term 1 Test A

Spelling script

Spelling 1: The word is **accommodate**.
We had to **accommodate** the extra guest in the caravan.
The word is **accommodate**.

Spelling 2: The word is **available**.
The boy was **available** to play in the match.
The word is **available**.

Spelling 3: The word is **competition**.
The **competition** was tough to play the lead role in the play.
The word is **competition**.

Spelling 4: The word is **determined**.
She was **determined** to prove her mum wrong.
The word is **determined**.

Spelling 5: The word is **excellent**.
The boy had an **excellent** school report again.
The word is **excellent**.

Spelling 6: The word is **achieve**.
She was desperate to **achieve** top marks in the test.
The word is **achieve**.

Spelling 7: The word is **bargain**.
Mum found an absolute **bargain** at the market.
The word is **bargain**.

Spelling 8: The word is **controversy**.
The penalty that was awarded caused huge **controversy**.
The word is **controversy**.

Spelling 9: The word is **disastrous**.
The avalanche had **disastrous** consequences for the ski resort.
The word is **disastrous**.

Spelling 10: The word is **familiar**.
The stranger at the back of the hall looked **familiar**.
The word is **familiar**.

Spelling 11: The word is **accidentally**.
She **accidentally** rode into the back of her friend's bike.
The word is **accidentally**.

Spelling 12: The word is **breathe**.
Sometimes it is hard to **breathe** when you have a cold.
The word is **breathe**.

Spelling 13: The word is **complete**.
Please **complete** the test to the best of your ability.
The word is **complete**.

Spelling 14: The word is **eight**.
The octopus squeezed each of its **eight** legs into the old jar in the tank.
The word is **eight**.

Spelling 15: The word is **forward**.
We inched **forward** slowly in the traffic jam.
The word is **forward**.

Spelling 16: The word is **address**.
Please **address** the letter in your best handwriting.
The word is **address**.

Spelling 17: The word is **business**.
"It's none of your **business**!" snapped the irritated teacher.
The word is **business**.

Spelling 18: The word is **decide**.
Please **decide** who you want to work with today.
The word is **decide**.

Spelling 19: The word is **exercise**.
Press ups are my least favourite **exercise**.
The word is **exercise**.

Spelling 20: The word is **group**.
The **group** of teenagers played at the skate park.
The word is **group**.

Well done! Now I will read the sentences again so you can check your spelling.

© HarperCollins*Publishers* Ltd 2018

| Name | Class | Date |

Year 6/P7 Autumn Half Term 1 Test A

1. We had to _____ the extra guest in the caravan.

2. The boy was _____ to play in the match.

3. The _____ was tough to play the lead role in the play.

4. She was _____ to prove her mum wrong.

5. The boy had an _____ school report again.

6. She was desperate to _____ top marks in the test.

7. Mum found an absolute _____ at the market.

8. The penalty that was awarded caused huge _____.

9. The avalanche had _____ consequences for the ski resort.

10. The stranger at the back of the hall looked _____.

11. She _____ rode into the back of her friend's bike.

12. Sometimes it is hard to _____ when you have a cold.

13. Please _____ the test to the best of your ability.

14. The octopus squeezed each of its _____ legs into the old jar in the tank.

15. We inched _____ slowly in the traffic jam.

16. Please _____ the letter in your best handwriting.

17. "It's none of your _____!" snapped the irritated teacher.

18. Please _____ who you want to work with today.

19. Press ups are my least favourite _____.

20. The _____ of teenagers played at the skate park.

Total _____ / 20

Year 6/P7 Autumn Half Term 1 Test B

Spelling rules and knowledge

- The words in this test can be used to check knowledge of the words from the statutory word lists for Years 3 to 6. Words from Years 3 and 4 are included for revision.

Guidance for teachers

The test is designed to build experience and confidence with this format, as well as to test children's spelling knowledge.
The test should take approximately 15 minutes.
Children should have a copy of the test and a pencil to use.
Children with specific needs should be given appropriate support.
All children should be encouraged to have a go at spelling each word, using the strategies that they have learnt.
Remind the children to check their answers by asking: *Does it look right? Does it sound right? Does it make sense in the sentence?*
Avoid over-emphasising the spelling of each word as you read it.

> Read each word aloud, saying: *The word is…*
> Next, read the sentence that includes the word.
> Wait for the children to attempt to write the word.
> Re-read the word, saying: *The word is…*

Remind the children to check the word before moving to the next spelling.
At the end of the test, read each sentence again and encourage the children to check back.

Instructions for children

(You may like to read this to the children prior to the test.)

This is a spelling test to check your knowledge of the spelling words we have worked on.
You need a pencil.
Please write your name, class and the date at the top of the test.
I will read a word out loud and then say it again in a sentence.
You should write the word in the gap in the sentence on your test.
I will read it again and give you time to check it.
Don't worry if you are not sure about a spelling. Have a go using the strategies we have learnt.
If you make a mistake, cross out the word and try again.

Words tested (20)

accompany, average, conscience, develop, existence, aggressive, bruise, convenience, embarrass, foreign, actual, build, consider, eighth, fruit, actually, busy, continue, enough, grammar

Year 6/P7 Autumn Half Term 1 Test B

Spelling script

Spelling 1: The word is **accompany**.
We wanted to **accompany** our guest at all times.
The word is **accompany**.

Spelling 2: The word is **average**.
The **average** number of hours that people sleep for each night is eight.
The word is **average**.

Spelling 3: The word is **conscience**.
It was on his **conscience** that he had told a lie.
The word is **conscience**.

Spelling 4: The word is **develop**.
Please can you **develop** your answer further?
The word is **develop**.

Spelling 5: The word is **existence**.
The **existence** of dinosaurs has been proved by their fossils and skeletons.
The word is **existence**.

Spelling 6: The word is **aggressive**.
The **aggressive** hound snarled at the police officer.
The word is **aggressive**.

Spelling 7: The word is **bruise**.
The **bruise** on my hip stopped me getting to sleep.
The word is **bruise**.

Spelling 8: The word is **convenience**.
The **convenience** store sold food and drinks from 7:00 a.m. to 11:00 p.m.
The word is **convenience**.

Spelling 9: The word is **embarrass**.
"Please try not to **embarrass** me!" the girl said to her mum.
The word is **embarrass**.

Spelling 10: The word is **foreign**.
We are so excited to be going on a **foreign** holiday.
The word is **foreign**.

Spelling 11: The word is **actual**.
The **actual** time that the sun rose was 7:00 a.m.
The word is **actual**.

Spelling 12: The word is **build**.
Let's **build** a den in the woods.
The word is **build**.

Spelling 13: The word is **consider**.
It is important to **consider** your teammates' feelings.
The word is **consider**.

Spelling 14: The word is **eighth**.
Neptune is the **eighth** planet in distance from the sun.
The word is **eighth**.

Spelling 15: The word is **fruit**.
The **fruit** bowl contained a pineapple and a mango.
The word is **fruit**.

Spelling 16: The word is **actually**.
He **actually** deserved to win the race, even though he tripped at the last stage.
The word is **actually**.

Spelling 17: The word is **busy**.
The city gets so **busy** on Saturdays.
The word is **busy**.

Spelling 18: The word is **continue**.
Please **continue** to read quietly to the end.
The word is **continue**.

Spelling 19: The word is **enough**.
Are there **enough** chairs for everyone?
The word is **enough**.

Spelling 20: The word is **grammar**.
My dad helps me with my **grammar** homework.
The word is **grammar**.

Well done! Now I will read the sentences again so you can check your spelling.

| Name | Class | Date |

Year 6/P7 Autumn Half Term 1 Test B

1. We wanted to _____ our guest at all times.

2. The _____ number of hours that people sleep for each night is eight.

3. It was on his _____ that he had told a lie.

4. Please can you _____ your answer further?

5. The _____ of dinosaurs has been proved by their fossils and skeletons.

6. The _____ hound snarled at the police officer.

7. The _____ on my hip stopped me getting to sleep.

8. The _____ store sold food and drinks from 7:00 a.m. to 11:00 p.m.

9. "Please try not to _____ me!" the girl said to her mum.

10. We are so excited to be going on a _____ holiday.

11. The _____ time that the sun rose was 7:00 a.m.

12. Let's _____ a den in the woods.

13. It is important to _____ your teammates' feelings.

14. Neptune is the _____ planet in distance from the sun.

15. The _____ bowl contained a pineapple and a mango.

16. He _____ deserved to win the race, even though he tripped at the last stage.

17. The city gets so _____ on Saturdays.

18. Please _____ to read quietly to the end.

19. Are there _____ chairs for everyone?

20. My dad helps me with my _____ homework.

Total _____ / 20

Year 6/P7 Autumn Half Term 2 Test A

Spelling rules and knowledge

- The words in this test can be used to check knowledge of the words from the statutory word lists for Years 3 to 6. Words from Years 3 and 4 are included for revision.

Guidance for teachers

The test is designed to build experience and confidence with this format, as well as to test children's spelling knowledge.
The test should take approximately 15 minutes.
Children should have a copy of the test and a pencil to use.
Children with specific needs should be given appropriate support.
All children should be encouraged to have a go at spelling each word, using the strategies that they have learnt.
Remind the children to check their answers by asking: *Does it look right? Does it sound right? Does it make sense in the sentence?*
Avoid over-emphasising the spelling of each word as you read it.

> Read each word aloud, saying: *The word is…*
> Next, read the sentence that includes the word.
> Wait for the children to attempt to write the word.
> Re-read the word, saying: *The word is…*

Remind the children to check the word before moving to the next spelling.
At the end of the test, read each sentence again and encourage the children to check back.

Instructions for children

(You may like to read this to the children prior to the test.)

This is a spelling test to check your knowledge of the spelling words we have worked on.
You need a pencil.
Please write your name, class and the date at the top of the test.
I will read a word out loud and then say it again in a sentence.
You should write the word in the gap in the sentence on your test.
I will read it again and give you time to check it.
Don't worry if you are not sure about a spelling. Have a go using the strategies we have learnt.
If you make a mistake, cross out the word and try again.

Words tested (20)

apparent, committee, curiosity, equipment, government, attached, community, desperate, exaggerate, harass, answer, calendar, describe, experience, guard, arrive, centre, difficult, extreme, heard

Year 6/P7 Autumn Half Term 2 Test A

Spelling script

Spelling 1: The word is **apparent**.
It was **apparent** that he was out of breath.
The word is **apparent**.

Spelling 2: The word is **committee**.
The **committee** decided to appoint a new chairperson.
The word is **committee**.

Spelling 3: The word is **curiosity**.
His **curiosity** got the better of him!
The word is **curiosity**.

Spelling 4: The word is **equipment**.
Our camping **equipment** was ready to pack.
The word is **equipment**.

Spelling 5: The word is **government**.
The **government** changed after the election.
The word is **government**.

Spelling 6: The word is **attached**.
I am very **attached** to my family and friends.
The word is **attached**.

Spelling 7: The word is **community**.
We are building a new **community** playground for the children.
The word is **community**.

Spelling 8: The word is **desperate**.
She was **desperate** for a drink after the race.
The word is **desperate**.

Spelling 9: The word is **exaggerate**.
The fisherman liked to **exaggerate** about the size of his catch.
The word is **exaggerate**.

Spelling 10: The word is **harass**.
It's important not to **harass** a new pet but to let it settle.
The word is **harass**.

Spelling 11: The word is **answer**.
If you know the **answer**, please put up your hand.
The word is **answer**.

Spelling 12: The word is **calendar**.
We keep a record of our guitar lessons on the **calendar**.
The word is **calendar**.

Spelling 13: The word is **describe**.
He had to try to **describe** the thief's appearance to the detective.
The word is **describe**.

Spelling 14: The word is **experience**.
Your first residential trip can be a daunting **experience**.
The word is **experience**.

Spelling 15: The word is **guard**.
The **guard** dog growled at the intruder.
The word is **guard**.

Spelling 16: The word is **arrive**.
Please **arrive** punctually at 6:00 p.m.
The word is **arrive**.

Spelling 17: The word is **centre**.
The sports **centre** had a new gymnasium.
The word is **centre**.

Spelling 18: The word is **difficult**.
It is **difficult** for some people to stand on their head.
The word is **difficult**.

Spelling 19: The word is **extreme**.
The **extreme** weather meant we couldn't leave the house.
The word is **extreme**.

Spelling 20: The word is **heard**.
We **heard** the whistle but carried on playing anyway!
The word is **heard**.

Well done! Now I will read the sentences again so you can check your spelling.

| Name | Class | Date |

Year 6/P7 Autumn Half Term 2 Test A

1. It was _____ that he was out of breath.

2. The _____ decided to appoint a new chairperson.

3. His _____ got the better of him!

4. Our camping _____ was ready to pack.

5. The _____ changed after the election.

6. I am very _____ to my family and friends.

7. We are building a new _____ playground for the children.

8. She was _____ for a drink after the race.

9. The fisherman liked to _____ about the size of his catch.

10. It's important not to _____ a new pet but to let it settle.

11. If you know the _____, please put up your hand.

12. We keep a record of our guitar lessons on the _____.

13. He had to try to _____ the thief's appearance to the detective.

14. Your first residential trip can be a daunting _____.

15. The _____ dog growled at the intruder.

16. Please _____ punctually at 6:00 p.m.

17. The sports _____ had a new gymnasium.

18. It is _____ for some people to stand on their head.

19. The _____ weather meant we couldn't leave the house.

20. We _____ the whistle but carried on playing anyway!

Total _____ / 20

Year 6/P7 Autumn Half Term 2 Test B

Spelling rules and knowledge

- The words in this test can be used to check knowledge of the words from the statutory word lists for Years 3 to 6. Words from Years 3 and 4 are included for revision.

Guidance for teachers

The test is designed to build experience and confidence with this format, as well as to test children's spelling knowledge.
The test should take approximately 15 minutes.
Children should have a copy of the test and a pencil to use.
Children with specific needs should be given appropriate support.
All children should be encouraged to have a go at spelling each word, using the strategies that they have learnt.
Remind the children to check their answers by asking: *Does it look right? Does it sound right? Does it make sense in the sentence?*
Avoid over-emphasising the spelling of each word as you read it.

    Read each word aloud, saying: *The word is…*
    Next, read the sentence that includes the word.
    Wait for the children to attempt to write the word.
    Re-read the word, saying: *The word is…*

Remind the children to check the word before moving to the next spelling.
At the end of the test, read each sentence again and encourage the children to check back.

Instructions for children

(You may like to read this to the children prior to the test.)

This is a spelling test to check your knowledge of the spelling words we have worked on.
You need a pencil.
Please write your name, class and the date at the top of the test.
I will read a word out loud and then say it again in a sentence.
You should write the word in the gap in the sentence on your test.
I will read it again and give you time to check it.
Don't worry if you are not sure about a spelling. Have a go using the strategies we have learnt.
If you make a mistake, cross out the word and try again.

Words tested (20)

amateur, category, correspond, environment, forty, appreciate, communicate, definite, especially, guarantee, appear, caught, different, experiment, guide, believe, century, disappear, famous, heart

Year 6/P7 Autumn Half Term 2 Test B

Spelling script

Spelling 1: The word is **amateur**.
The **amateur** boxer dreaded entering the ring.
The word is **amateur**.

Spelling 2: The word is **category**.
She competed in the swimming gala for her age **category**.
The word is **category**.

Spelling 3: The word is **correspond**.
We sometimes **correspond** by email; sometimes by letter.
The word is **correspond**.

Spelling 4: The word is **environment**.
We can make our **environment** more pleasant by planting flowers.
The word is **environment**.

Spelling 5: The word is **forty**.
When Dad was **forty**, we had a big party.
The word is **forty**.

Spelling 6: The word is **appreciate**.
He didn't **appreciate** the effort they had made.
The word is **appreciate**.

Spelling 7: The word is **communicate**.
They tried to **communicate** using sign language.
The word is **communicate**.

Spelling 8: The word is **definite**.
He made a **definite** offer in the auction.
The word is **definite**.

Spelling 9: The word is **especially**.
The apple pie was **especially** sweet.
The word is **especially**.

Spelling 10: The word is **guarantee**.
The **guarantee** expired the day before the washing machine broke down.
The word is **guarantee**.

Spelling 11: The word is **appear**.
The birds didn't **appear**, even though we watched all afternoon.
The word is **appear**.

Spelling 12: The word is **caught**.
She **caught** a cold on her birthday!
The word is **caught**.

Spelling 13: The word is **different**.
We go to bed at **different** times in the holidays.
The word is **different**.

Spelling 14: The word is **experiment**.
The science **experiment** went disastrously wrong.
The word is **experiment**.

Spelling 15: The word is **guide**.
They hired a **guide** to help them tour the famous sites.
The word is **guide**.

Spelling 16: The word is **believe**.
He couldn't **believe** how much money it cost.
The word is **believe**.

Spelling 17: The word is **century**.
We live in the twenty-first **century**.
The word is **century**.

Spelling 18: The word is **disappear**.
We watched the dolphins **disappear** beneath the waves.
The word is **disappear**.

Spelling 19: The word is **famous**.
The **famous** footballer scored a hat-trick in the first half.
The word is **famous**.

Spelling 20: The word is **heart**.
Your **heart** pumps blood around your body.
The word is **heart**.

Well done! Now I will read the sentences again so you can check your spelling.

| Name | Class | Date |

Year 6/P7 Autumn Half Term 2 Test B

1. The _____ boxer dreaded entering the ring.

2. She competed in the swimming gala for her age _____.

3. We sometimes _____ by email; sometimes by letter.

4. We can make our _____ more pleasant by planting flowers.

5. When Dad was _____, we had a big party.

6. He didn't _____ the effort they had made.

7. They tried to _____ using sign language.

8. He made a _____ offer in the auction.

9. The apple pie was _____ sweet.

10. The _____ expired the day before the washing machine broke down.

11. The birds didn't _____, even though we watched all afternoon.

12. She _____ a cold on her birthday!

13. We go to bed at _____ times in the holidays.

14. The science _____ went disastrously wrong.

15. They hired a _____ to help them tour the famous sites.

16. He couldn't _____ how much money it cost.

17. We live in the twenty-first _____.

18. We watched the dolphins _____ beneath the waves.

19. The _____ footballer scored a hat-trick in the first half.

20. Your _____ pumps blood around your body.

Total _____ / 20

Year 6/P7 Spring Half Term 1 Test A

Spelling rules and knowledge

- The words in this test can be used to check knowledge of the words from the statutory word lists for Years 3 to 6. Words from Years 3 and 4 are included for revision.

Guidance for teachers

The test is designed to build experience and confidence with this format, as well as to test children's spelling knowledge.
The test should take approximately 15 minutes.
Children should have a copy of the test and a pencil to use.
Children with specific needs should be given appropriate support.
All children should be encouraged to have a go at spelling each word, using the strategies that they have learnt.
Remind the children to check their answers by asking: *Does it look right? Does it sound right? Does it make sense in the sentence?*
Avoid over-emphasising the spelling of each word as you read it.

> Read each word aloud, saying: *The word is…*
> Next, read the sentence that includes the word.
> Wait for the children to attempt to write the word.
> Re-read the word, saying: *The word is…*

Remind the children to check the word before moving to the next spelling.
At the end of the test, read each sentence again and encourage the children to check back.

Instructions for children

(You may like to read this to the children prior to the test.)

This is a spelling test to check your knowledge of the spelling words we have worked on.
You need a pencil.
Please write your name, class and the date at the top of the test.
I will read a word out loud and then say it again in a sentence.
You should write the word in the gap in the sentence on your test.
I will read it again and give you time to check it.
Don't worry if you are not sure about a spelling. Have a go using the strategies we have learnt.
If you make a mistake, cross out the word and try again.

Words tested (20)

hindrance, marvellous, persuade, relevant, soldier, immediately, necessary, privilege, rhythm, suggest, imagine, medicine, ordinary, pressure, sentence, interest, natural, perhaps, purpose, straight

Year 6/P7 Spring Half Term 1 Test A

Spelling script

Spelling 1: The word is **hindrance**.
My little sister was a real **hindrance** on the bike ride.
The word is **hindrance**.

Spelling 2: The word is **marvellous**.
The trip to the film studios was a **marvellous** treat.
The word is **marvellous**.

Spelling 3: The word is **persuade**.
The girl tried to **persuade** her sister to eat a spider.
The word is **persuade**.

Spelling 4: The word is **relevant**.
He made a **relevant** contribution to the discussion.
The word is **relevant**.

Spelling 5: The word is **soldier**.
The eager **soldier** volunteered to lead the march.
The word is **soldier**.

Spelling 6: The word is **immediately**.
Please respond **immediately** if you hear the siren.
The word is **immediately**.

Spelling 7: The word is **necessary**.
It is not **necessary** to wear your hat and scarf today.
The word is **necessary**.

Spelling 8: The word is **privilege**.
It has been a **privilege** to be here today.
The word is **privilege**.

Spelling 9: The word is **rhythm**.
The drummer had an outstanding sense of **rhythm**.
The word is **rhythm**.

Spelling 10: The word is **suggest**.
I **suggest** you come running tomorrow.
The word is **suggest**.

Spelling 11: The word is **imagine**.
He tried to **imagine** life without ice cream.
The word is **imagine**.

Spelling 12: The word is **medicine**.
The **medicine** had the most appalling flavour.
The word is **medicine**.

Spelling 13: The word is **ordinary**.
It soon became apparent that he was no **ordinary** guitar player.
The word is **ordinary**.

Spelling 14: The word is **pressure**.
The **pressure** in her bicycle tyres was too low, so she had to pump them up.
The word is **pressure**.

Spelling 15: The word is **sentence**.
The man had to serve a 20-year **sentence** in prison.
The word is **sentence**.

Spelling 16: The word is **interest**.
The children had little **interest** in the choice of activities on offer.
The word is **interest**.

Spelling 17: The word is **natural**.
The Grand Canyon is a **natural** wonder.
The word is **natural**.

Spelling 18: The word is **perhaps**.
Perhaps you would like to try skating today.
The word is **perhaps**.

Spelling 19: The word is **purpose**.
She trod on her brother's toe on **purpose**.
The word is **purpose**.

Spelling 20: The word is **straight**.
The boy drew a completely **straight** line with his ruler.
The word is **straight**.

Well done! Now I will read the sentences again so you can check your spelling.

© HarperCollins*Publishers* Ltd 2018

| Name | Class | Date |

Year 6/P7 Spring Half Term 1 Test A

1. My little sister was a real _____ on the bike ride.

2. The trip to the film studios was a _____ treat.

3. The girl tried to _____ her sister to eat a spider.

4. He made a _____ contribution to the discussion.

5. The eager _____ volunteered to lead the march.

6. Please respond _____ if you hear the siren.

7. It is not _____ to wear your hat and scarf today.

8. It has been a _____ to be here today.

9. The drummer had an outstanding sense of _____.

10. I _____ you come running tomorrow.

11. He tried to _____ life without ice cream.

12. The _____ had the most appalling flavour.

13. It soon became apparent that he was no _____ guitar player.

14. The _____ in her bicycle tyres was too low, so she had to pump them up.

15. The man had to serve a 20-year _____ in prison.

16. The children had little _____ in the choice of activities on offer.

17. The Grand Canyon is a _____ wonder.

18. _____ you would like to try skating today.

19. She trod on her brother's toe on _____.

20. The boy drew a completely _____ line with his ruler.

Total _____ / 20

Year 6/P7 Spring Half Term 1 Test B

Spelling rules and knowledge

- The words in this test can be used to check knowledge of the words from the statutory word lists for Years 3 to 6. Words from Years 3 and 4 are included for revision.

Guidance for teachers

The test is designed to build experience and confidence with this format, as well as to test children's spelling knowledge.
The test should take approximately 15 minutes.
Children should have a copy of the test and a pencil to use.
Children with specific needs should be given appropriate support.
All children should be encouraged to have a go at spelling each word, using the strategies that they have learnt.
Remind the children to check their answers by asking: *Does it look right? Does it sound right? Does it make sense in the sentence?*
Avoid over-emphasising the spelling of each word as you read it.

> Read each word aloud, saying: *The word is…*
> Next, read the sentence that includes the word.
> Wait for the children to attempt to write the word.
> Re-read the word, saying: *The word is…*

Remind the children to check the word before moving to the next spelling.
At the end of the test, read each sentence again and encourage the children to check back.

Instructions for children

(You may like to read this to the children prior to the test.)

This is a spelling test to check your knowledge of the spelling words we have worked on.
You need a pencil.
Please write your name, class and the date at the top of the test.
I will read a word out loud and then say it again in a sentence.
You should write the word in the gap in the sentence on your test.
I will read it again and give you time to check it.
Don't worry if you are not sure about a spelling. Have a go using the strategies we have learnt.
If you make a mistake, cross out the word and try again.

Words tested (20)

identity, mischievous, physical, restaurant, stomach, individual, neighbour, profession, sacrifice, symbol, increase, mention, particular, probably, separate, important, minute, peculiar, promise, special

Year 6/P7 Spring Half Term 1 Test B

Spelling script

Spelling 1: The word is **identity**.
We competed to work out the **identity** of the murderer in the game.
The word is **identity**.

Spelling 2: The word is **mischievous**.
The **mischievous** kitten would not come inside.
The word is **mischievous**.

Spelling 3: The word is **physical**.
She had to pass a **physical** test to get into the army.
The word is **physical**.

Spelling 4: The word is **restaurant**.
The French **restaurant** served snails in garlic.
The word is **restaurant**.

Spelling 5: The word is **stomach**.
His **stomach** ache stopped him from running the cross-country course.
The word is **stomach**.

Spelling 6: The word is **individual**.
Each **individual** statue had a different expression.
The word is **individual**.

Spelling 7: The word is **neighbour**.
My **neighbour** fed my hamster when I was away.
The word is **neighbour**.

Spelling 8: The word is **profession**.
The dentist considered her **profession** to be worthy.
The word is **profession**.

Spelling 9: The word is **sacrifice**.
The tribespeople might **sacrifice** one of their animals in a ceremony.
The word is **sacrifice**.

Spelling 10: The word is **symbol**.
An emoji is a **symbol** that communicates a message.
The word is **symbol**.

Spelling 11: The word is **increase**.
We watched the water inside our rowing boat **increase** as we rowed across the lake.
The word is **increase**.

Spelling 12: The word is **mention**.
He tried not to **mention** the bad news.
The word is **mention**.

Spelling 13: The word is **particular**.
She was extremely agitated on that **particular** day.
The word is **particular**.

Spelling 14: The word is **probably**.
I could **probably** make it to the train station on time.
The word is **probably**.

Spelling 15: The word is **separate**.
Try not to become **separate** from the rest of the group.
The word is **separate**.

Spelling 16: The word is **important**.
He carried the **important** letter inside his jacket.
The word is **important**.

Spelling 17: The word is **minute**.
In one **minute**, there are sixty seconds.
The word is **minute**.

Spelling 18: The word is **peculiar**.
The strange potion made her feel extremely **peculiar**.
The word is **peculiar**.

Spelling 19: The word is **promise**.
If I make a **promise**, then I will keep it.
The word is **promise**.

Spelling 20: The word is **special**.
My birthday is always a **special** day.
The word is **special**.

Well done! Now I will read the sentences again so you can check your spelling.

| Name | Class | Date |

Year 6/P7 Spring Half Term 1 Test B

1. We competed to work out the _____ of the murderer in the game.

2. The _____ kitten would not come inside.

3. She had to pass a _____ test to get into the army.

4. The French _____ served snails in garlic.

5. His _____ ache stopped him from running the cross-country course.

6. Each _____ statue had a different expression.

7. My _____ fed my hamster when I was away.

8. The dentist considered her _____ to be worthy.

9. The tribespeople might _____ one of their animals in a ceremony.

10. An emoji is a _____ that communicates a message.

11. We watched the water inside our rowing boat _____ as we rowed across the lake.

12. He tried not to _____ the bad news.

13. She was extremely agitated on that _____ day.

14. I could _____ make it to the train station on time.

15. Try not to become _____ from the rest of the group.

16. He carried the _____ letter inside his jacket.

17. In one _____, there are sixty seconds.

18. The strange potion made her feel extremely _____.

19. If I make a _____, then I will keep it.

20. My birthday is always a _____ day.

Total _____ / 20

Year 6/P7 Spring Half Term 2 Test A

Spelling rules and knowledge

- The words in this test can be used to check knowledge of the words from the statutory word lists for Years 3 to 6. Words from Years 3 and 4 are included for revision.

Guidance for teachers

The test is designed to build experience and confidence with this format, as well as to test children's spelling knowledge.
The test should take approximately 15 minutes.
Children should have a copy of the test and a pencil to use.
Children with specific needs should be given appropriate support.
All children should be encouraged to have a go at spelling each word, using the strategies that they have learnt.
Remind the children to check their answers by asking: *Does it look right? Does it sound right? Does it make sense in the sentence?*
Avoid over-emphasising the spelling of each word as you read it.

> Read each word aloud, saying: *The word is…*
> Next, read the sentence that includes the word.
> Wait for the children to attempt to write the word.
> Re-read the word, saying: *The word is…*

Remind the children to check the word before moving to the next spelling.
At the end of the test, read each sentence again and encourage the children to check back.

Instructions for children

(You may like to read this to the children prior to the test.)

This is a spelling test to check your knowledge of the spelling words we have worked on.
You need a pencil.
Please write your name, class and the date at the top of the test.
I will read a word out loud and then say it again in a sentence.
You should write the word in the gap in the sentence on your test.
I will read it again and give you time to check it.
Don't worry if you are not sure about a spelling. Have a go using the strategies we have learnt.
If you make a mistake, cross out the word and try again.

Words tested (20)

language, occur, queue, signature, thorough, lightning, parliament, recommend, sincerely, variety, island, naughty, popular, quarter, strange, learn, occasion, possess, recent, suppose

Year 6/P7 Spring Half Term 2 Test A

Spelling script

Spelling 1: The word is **language**.
The stranger was speaking in a foreign **language**.
The word is **language**.

Spelling 2: The word is **occur**.
Multiples of 10 **occur** alternately in the 5 times table.
The word is **occur**.

Spelling 3: The word is **queue**.
We had to **queue** for an ice cream.
The word is **queue**.

Spelling 4: The word is **signature**.
I have been practising writing my **signature**.
The word is **signature**.

Spelling 5: The word is **thorough**.
The search for the missing socks was very **thorough**.
The word is **thorough**.

Spelling 6: The word is **lightning**.
Thunder usually booms a few seconds after **lightning** has flashed.
The word is **lightning**.

Spelling 7: The word is **parliament**.
The Houses of **Parliament** are in central London.
The word is **parliament**.

Spelling 8: The word is **recommend**.
The librarian could **recommend** great new authors to try.
The word is **recommend**.

Spelling 9: The word is **sincerely**.
He was **sincerely** sorry for the trouble he caused.
The word is **sincerely**.

Spelling 10: The word is **variety**.
There was a great **variety** of vegetables in the market.
The word is **variety**.

Spelling 11: The word is **island**.
The **island** looked beautiful from the plane window.
The word is **island**.

Spelling 12: The word is **naughty**.
The **naughty** children had to stay in at lunchtime.
The word is **naughty**.

Spelling 13: The word is **popular**.
The most **popular** musician won all the prizes at the ceremony.
The word is **popular**.

Spelling 14: The word is **quarter**.
You can have a snack at **quarter** to eleven.
The word is **quarter**.

Spelling 15: The word is **strange**.
She had a **strange** premonition when she saw the gloomy old house.
The word is **strange**.

Spelling 16: The word is **learn**.
It is hard to **learn** a new skill when you are tired and hungry!
The word is **learn**.

Spelling 17: The word is **occasion**.
We wore our best clothes for the grand **occasion**.
The word is **occasion**.

Spelling 18: The word is **possess**.
I only **possess** one working handwriting pen!
The word is **possess**.

Spelling 19: The word is **recent**.
The **recent** film had attracted huge crowds to the cinema.
The word is **recent**.

Spelling 20: The word is **suppose**.
Do you **suppose** that I could have a cup of tea?
The word is **suppose**.

Well done! Now I will read the sentences again so you can check your spelling.

| Name | Class | Date |

Year 6/P7 Spring Half Term 2 Test A

1. The stranger was speaking in a foreign _____.

2. Multiples of 10 _____ alternately in the 5 times table.

3. We had to _____ for an ice cream.

4. I have been practising writing my _____.

5. The search for the missing socks was very _____.

6. Thunder usually booms a few seconds after _____ has flashed.

7. The Houses of _____ are in central London.

8. The librarian could _____ great new authors to try.

9. He was _____ sorry for the trouble he caused.

10. There was a great _____ of vegetables in the market.

11. The _____ looked beautiful from the plane window.

12. The _____ children had to stay in at lunchtime.

13. The most _____ musician won all the prizes at the ceremony.

14. You can have a snack at _____ to eleven.

15. She had a _____ premonition when she saw the gloomy old house.

16. It is hard to _____ a new skill when you are tired and hungry!

17. We wore our best clothes for the grand _____.

18. I only _____ one working handwriting pen!

19. The _____ film had attracted huge crowds to the cinema.

20. Do you _____ that I could have a cup of tea?

Total _____ / 20

Year 6/P7 Spring Half Term 2 Test B

Spelling rules and knowledge

- The words in this test can be used to check knowledge of the words from the statutory word lists for Years 3 to 6. Words from Years 3 and 4 are included for revision.

Guidance for teachers

The test is designed to build experience and confidence with this format, as well as to test children's spelling knowledge.
The test should take approximately 15 minutes.
Children should have a copy of the test and a pencil to use.
Children with specific needs should be given appropriate support.
All children should be encouraged to have a go at spelling each word, using the strategies that they have learnt.
Remind the children to check their answers by asking: *Does it look right? Does it sound right? Does it make sense in the sentence?*
Avoid over-emphasising the spelling of each word as you read it.

> Read each word aloud, saying: *The word is…*
> Next, read the sentence that includes the word.
> Wait for the children to attempt to write the word.
> Re-read the word, saying: *The word is…*

Remind the children to check the word before moving to the next spelling.
At the end of the test, read each sentence again and encourage the children to check back.

Instructions for children

(You may like to read this to the children prior to the test.)

This is a spelling test to check your knowledge of the spelling words we have worked on.
You need a pencil.
Please write your name, class and the date at the top of the test.
I will read a word out loud and then say it again in a sentence.
You should write the word in the gap in the sentence on your test.
I will read it again and give you time to check it.
Don't worry if you are not sure about a spelling. Have a go using the strategies we have learnt.
If you make a mistake, cross out the word and try again.

Words tested (20)

interfere, nuisance, programme, secretary, system, leisure, opportunity, recognise, sincere, twelfth, knowledge, notice, position, question, strength, length, occasionally, possession, regular, surprise

Year 6/P7 Spring Half Term 2 Test B

Spelling script

Spelling 1: The word is **interfere**.
Please do not **interfere** with the computer while it is updating.
The word is **interfere**.

Spelling 2: The word is **nuisance**.
The wasps were a terrible **nuisance** at the picnic.
The word is **nuisance**.

Spelling 3: The word is **programme**.
Her favourite television **programme** was cancelled due to the breaking news.
The word is **programme**.

Spelling 4: The word is **secretary**.
Her **secretary** sent an email to cancel the meeting.
The word is **secretary**.

Spelling 5: The word is **system**.
The new booking **system** was a huge success.
The word is **system**.

Spelling 6: The word is **leisure**.
At the **leisure** centre, there are three trampolines.
The word is **leisure**.

Spelling 7: The word is **opportunity**.
The **opportunity** to hold the python was exciting!
The word is **opportunity**.

Spelling 8: The word is **recognise**.
He didn't **recognise** his sister after so many years apart.
The word is **recognise**.

Spelling 9: The word is **sincere**.
He gave his **sincere** apologies for missing the special dinner party.
The word is **sincere**.

Spelling 10: The word is **twelfth**.
The **twelfth** month of the year is December.
The word is **twelfth**.

Spelling 11: The word is **knowledge**.
Knowledge may be recorded in encyclopaedias.
The word is **knowledge**.

Spelling 12: The word is **notice**.
The **notice** was pinned up where it could not be missed.
The word is **notice**.

Spelling 13: The word is **position**.
Her **position** in the league table dropped from second to third.
The word is **position**.

Spelling 14: The word is **question**.
The police officer was ready to **question** the thief.
The word is **question**.

Spelling 15: The word is **strength**.
Your **strength** will improve if you lift weights.
The word is **strength**.

Spelling 16: The word is **length**.
Each **length** of the swimming pool made his arms more tired.
The word is **length**.

Spelling 17: The word is **occasionally**.
Occasionally we are allowed fizzy drinks with dinner.
The word is **occasionally**.

Spelling 18: The word is **possession**.
His most precious **possession** was his football shirt.
The word is **possession**.

Spelling 19: The word is **regular**.
She visited her granny on a **regular** basis.
The word is **regular**.

Spelling 20: The word is **surprise**.
The present was a wonderful **surprise**.
The word is **surprise**.

Well done! Now I will read the sentences again so you can check your spelling.

| Name | Class | Date |

Year 6/P7 Spring Half Term 2 Test B

1. Please do not _____ with the computer while it is updating.

2. The wasps were a terrible _____ at the picnic.

3. Her favourite television _____ was cancelled due to the breaking news.

4. Her _____ sent an email to cancel the meeting.

5. The new booking _____ was a huge success.

6. At the _____ centre, there are three trampolines.

7. The _____ to hold the python was exciting!

8. He didn't _____ his sister after so many years apart.

9. He gave his _____ apologies for missing the special dinner party.

10. The _____ month of the year is December.

11. _____ may be recorded in encyclopaedias.

12. The _____ was pinned up where it could not be missed.

13. Her _____ in the league table dropped from second to third.

14. The police officer was ready to _____ the thief.

15. Your _____ will improve if you lift weights.

16. Each _____ of the swimming pool made his arms more tired.

17. _____ we are allowed fizzy drinks with dinner.

18. His most precious _____ was his football shirt.

19. She visited her granny on a _____ basis.

20. The present was a wonderful _____.

Total _____ / 20

Year 6/P7 Summer Half Term 1 Test A

Spelling rules and knowledge

- The words in this test can be used to check knowledge of the words from the statutory word lists for Years 3 to 6. Words from Years 3 and 4 are included for revision.
- The words can also be used to revise content from the spelling rules for Years 3 and 4.

Guidance for teachers

The test is designed to build experience and confidence with this format, as well as to test children's spelling knowledge.

The test should take approximately 15 minutes.

Children should have a copy of the test and a pencil to use.

Children with specific needs should be given appropriate support.

All children should be encouraged to have a go at spelling each word, using the strategies that they have learnt.

Remind the children to check their answers by asking: *Does it look right? Does it sound right? Does it make sense in the sentence?*

Avoid over-emphasising the spelling of each word as you read it.

> Read each word aloud, saying: *The word is…*
> Next, read the sentence that includes the word.
> Wait for the children to attempt to write the word.
> Re-read the word, saying: *The word is…*

Remind the children to check the word before moving to the next spelling.
At the end of the test, read each sentence again and encourage the children to check back.

Instructions for children

(You may like to read this to the children prior to the test.)

This is a spelling test to check your knowledge of the spelling words we have worked on.
You need a pencil.
Please write your name, class and the date at the top of the test.
I will read a word out loud and then say it again in a sentence.
You should write the word in the gap in the sentence on your test.
I will read it again and give you time to check it.
Don't worry if you are not sure about a spelling. Have a go using the strategies we have learnt.
If you make a mistake, cross out the word and try again.

Words tested (20)

vegetable, forgotten, disagree, reappear, information, though, preferred, misheard, subtitle, usually, through, mystery, illegal, international, measure, woman, double, irrelevant, automatic, teacher

Year 6/P7 Summer Half Term 1 Test A

Spelling script

Spelling 1: The word is **vegetable**.
The rotten **vegetable** made the fridge smell terrible.
The word is **vegetable**.

Spelling 2: The word is **forgotten**.
She had **forgotten** to wear a sun hat again.
The word is **forgotten**.

Spelling 3: The word is **disagree**.
The boy would often **disagree** with his dad about his bedtime.
The word is **disagree**.

Spelling 4: The word is **reappear**.
We waited anxiously for our cat to **reappear**.
The word is **reappear**.

Spelling 5: The word is **information**.
The **information** was presented in a clear manner.
The word is **information**.

Spelling 6: The word is **though**.
Even **though** she was really hungry, she wouldn't eat the rice.
The word is **though**.

Spelling 7: The word is **preferred**.
The puppy **preferred** its smelly old blanket to the new cushion.
The word is **preferred**.

Spelling 8: The word is **misheard**.
She **misheard** the instructions and arrived ten minutes late.
The word is **misheard**.

Spelling 9: The word is **subtitle**.
The book's **subtitle** made it sound more interesting.
The word is **subtitle**.

Spelling 10: The word is **usually**.
He **usually** carried his own wetsuit to the beach.
The word is **usually**.

Spelling 11: The word is **through**.
He tried to squeeze **through** the hole in the fence.
The word is **through**.

Spelling 12: The word is **mystery**.
The famous **mystery** was a legend in their town.
The word is **mystery**.

Spelling 13: The word is **illegal**.
It is **illegal** to drive without a seatbelt.
The word is **illegal**.

Spelling 14: The word is **international**.
At the **international** tournament, players from every continent took part.
The word is **international**.

Spelling 15: The word is **measure**.
The tailor took care to **measure** the client precisely.
The word is **measure**.

Spelling 16: The word is **woman**.
The **woman** in the interview made a convincing argument for healthy eating.
The word is **woman**.

Spelling 17: The word is **double**.
I thought I was seeing **double** when I looked at the twins!
The word is **double**.

Spelling 18: The word is **irrelevant**.
Our report must not contain **irrelevant** information.
The word is **irrelevant**.

Spelling 19: The word is **automatic**.
Their promotion was **automatic** because they won the league.
The word is **automatic**.

Spelling 20: The word is **teacher**.
The **teacher** asked the children to work in pairs.
The word is **teacher**.

Well done! Now I will read the sentences again so you can check your spelling.

| Name | Class | Date |

Year 6/P7 Summer Half Term 1 Test A

1. The rotten _____ made the fridge smell terrible.

2. She had _____ to wear a sun hat again.

3. The boy would often _____ with his dad about his bedtime.

4. We waited anxiously for our cat to _____.

5. The _____ was presented in a clear manner.

6. Even _____ she was really hungry, she wouldn't eat the rice.

7. The puppy _____ its smelly old blanket to the new cushion.

8. She _____ the instructions and arrived ten minutes late.

9. The book's _____ made it sound more interesting.

10. He _____ carried his own wetsuit to the beach.

11. He tried to squeeze _____ the hole in the fence.

12. The famous _____ was a legend in their town.

13. It is _____ to drive without a seatbelt.

14. At the _____ tournament, players from every continent took part.

15. The tailor took care to _____ the client precisely.

16. The _____ in the interview made a convincing argument for healthy eating.

17. I thought I was seeing _____ when I looked at the twins!

18. Our report must not contain _____ information.

19. Their promotion was _____ because they won the league.

20. The _____ asked the children to work in pairs.

Total _____ / 20

Year 6/P7 Summer Half Term 1 Test B

Spelling rules and knowledge

- The words in this test can be used to check knowledge of the words from the statutory word lists for Years 3 to 6. Words from Years 3 and 4 are included for revision.
- The words can also be used to revise content from the spelling rules for Years 3 and 4.

Guidance for teachers

The test is designed to build experience and confidence with this format, as well as to test children's spelling knowledge.
The test should take approximately 15 minutes.
Children should have a copy of the test and a pencil to use.
Children with specific needs should be given appropriate support.
All children should be encouraged to have a go at spelling each word, using the strategies that they have learnt.
Remind the children to check their answers by asking: *Does it look right? Does it sound right? Does it make sense in the sentence?*
Avoid over-emphasising the spelling of each word as you read it.

> Read each word aloud, saying: *The word is…*
> Next, read the sentence that includes the word.
> Wait for the children to attempt to write the word.
> Re-read the word, saying: *The word is…*

Remind the children to check the word before moving to the next spelling.
At the end of the test, read each sentence again and encourage the children to check back.

Instructions for children

(You may like to read this to the children prior to the test.)

This is a spelling test to check your knowledge of the spelling words we have worked on.
You need a pencil.
Please write your name, class and the date at the top of the test.
I will read a word out loud and then say it again in a sentence.
You should write the word in the gap in the sentence on your test.
I will read it again and give you time to check it.
Don't worry if you are not sure about a spelling. Have a go using the strategies we have learnt.
If you make a mistake, cross out the word and try again.

Words tested (20)

vehicle, beginning, dishonest, rearrange, sensation, although, gardening, misfortune, superhuman, originally, various, sympathy, impossible, antiseptic, adventure, weight, touch, irresponsible, autograph, picture

Year 6/P7 Summer Half Term 1 Test B

Spelling script

Spelling 1: The word is **vehicle**.
Will the owner of the red **vehicle** please move it away from the entrance?
The word is **vehicle**.

Spelling 2: The word is **beginning**.
At the **beginning**, there was an eerie silence.
The word is **beginning**.

Spelling 3: The word is **dishonest**.
The **dishonest** tradesman was caught red-handed.
The word is **dishonest**.

Spelling 4: The word is **rearrange**.
I want to **rearrange** my bedroom furniture to make more space.
The word is **rearrange**.

Spelling 5: The word is **sensation**.
Flying through the air is a strange **sensation**.
The word is **sensation**.

Spelling 6: The word is **although**.
Although she was eager, she waited until last.
The word is **although**.

Spelling 7: The word is **gardening**.
The **gardening** chores were never-ending!
The word is **gardening**.

Spelling 8: The word is **misfortune**.
She had real **misfortune** when she lost her phone and bag on the same day.
The word is **misfortune**.

Spelling 9: The word is **superhuman**.
Some weightlifters appear to have **superhuman** strength.
The word is **superhuman**.

Spelling 10: The word is **originally**.
Originally, we were aiming to arrive at 1:00 p.m.
The word is **originally**.

Spelling 11: The word is **various**.
Of all the **various** birds in the garden, the goldfinch is my favourite.
The word is **various**.

Spelling 12: The word is **sympathy**.
He had my **sympathy** when he broke his finger.
The word is **sympathy**.

Spelling 13: The word is **impossible**.
Learning to ski seemed like an **impossible** challenge.
The word is **impossible**.

Spelling 14: The word is **antiseptic**.
Dad put **antiseptic** on my wound.
The word is **antiseptic**.

Spelling 15: The word is **adventure**.
The holiday promised to be a great **adventure**.
The word is **adventure**.

Spelling 16: The word is **weight**.
The baby elephant's **weight** had nearly doubled!
The word is **weight**.

Spelling 17: The word is **touch**.
You have to **touch** your ticket on the reader to open the barrier.
The word is **touch**.

Spelling 18: The word is **irresponsible**.
His **irresponsible** actions led to him being grounded!
The word is **irresponsible**.

Spelling 19: The word is **autograph**.
She treasured the actor's **autograph** forever.
The word is **autograph**.

Spelling 20: The word is **picture**.
Behind the **picture** there was a locked safe.
The word is **picture**.

Well done! Now I will read the sentences again so you can check your spelling.

| Name | Class | Date |

Year 6/P7 Summer Half Term 1 Test B

1. Will the owner of the red _____ please move it away from the entrance?

2. At the _____, there was an eerie silence.

3. The _____ tradesman was caught red-handed.

4. I want to _____ my bedroom furniture to make more space.

5. Flying through the air is a strange _____.

6. _____ she was eager, she waited until last.

7. The _____ chores were never-ending!

8. She had real _____ when she lost her phone and bag on the same day.

9. Some weightlifters appear to have _____ strength.

10. _____, we were aiming to arrive at 1:00 p.m.

11. Of all the _____ birds in the garden, the goldfinch is my favourite.

12. He had my _____ when he broke his finger.

13. Learning to ski seemed like an _____ challenge.

14. Dad put _____ on my wound.

15. The holiday promised to be a great _____.

16. The baby elephant's _____ had nearly doubled!

17. You have to _____ your ticket on the reader to open the barrier.

18. His _____ actions led to him being grounded!

19. She treasured the actor's _____ forever.

20. Behind the _____ there was a locked safe.

Total _____ / 20

Year 6/P7 Summer Half Term 2 Test A

Spelling rules and knowledge

- The words in this test can be used to revise content from the spelling rules for Years 3 and 4 and Years 5 and 6.

Guidance for teachers

The test is designed to build experience and confidence with this format, as well as to test children's spelling knowledge.
The test should take approximately 15 minutes.
Children should have a copy of the test and a pencil to use.
Children with specific needs should be given appropriate support.
All children should be encouraged to have a go at spelling each word, using the strategies that they have learnt.
Remind the children to check their answers by asking: *Does it look right? Does it sound right? Does it make sense in the sentence?*
Avoid over-emphasising the spelling of each word as you read it.

> Read each word aloud, saying: *The word is…*
> Next, read the sentence that includes the word.
> Wait for the children to attempt to write the word.
> Re-read the word, saying: *The word is…*

Remind the children to check the word before moving to the next spelling.
At the end of the test, read each sentence again and encourage the children to check back.

Instructions for children

(You may like to read this to the children prior to the test.)

This is a spelling test to check your knowledge of the spelling words we have worked on.
You need a pencil.
Please write your name, class and the date at the top of the test.
I will read a word out loud and then say it again in a sentence.
You should write the word in the gap in the sentence on your test.
I will read it again and give you time to check it.
Don't worry if you are not sure about a spelling. Have a go using the strategies we have learnt.
If you make a mistake, cross out the word and try again.

Words tested (20)

vigorous, chef, artificial, visibly, accept, rejection, plague, tolerance, transferring, alter, election, discipline, decency, receive, guessed, permission, neighbour, independence, brought, advise

Year 6/P7 Summer Half Term 2 Test A

Spelling script

Spelling 1: The word is **vigorous**.
The **vigorous** massage left the sports player ready for her next game.
The word is **vigorous**.

Spelling 2: The word is **chef**.
The top **chef** commanded perfection in his kitchen.
The word is **chef**.

Spelling 3: The word is **artificial**.
The **artificial** grass looked realistic.
The word is **artificial**.

Spelling 4: The word is **visibly**.
She was **visibly** upset by the terrible news.
The word is **visibly**.

Spelling 5: The word is **accept**.
She had to **accept** that the necklace might be lost forever.
The word is **accept**.

Spelling 6: The word is **rejection**.
The girl overcame her **rejection** from the audition and went on to be successful.
The word is **rejection**.

Spelling 7: The word is **plague**.
The **plague** in London was spread by fleas on rats.
The word is **plague**.

Spelling 8: The word is **tolerance**.
His **tolerance** of children improved when he started helping at school.
The word is **tolerance**.

Spelling 9: The word is **transferring**.
The data was **transferring** for hours!
The word is **transferring**.

Spelling 10: The word is **alter**.
Please do not **alter** the information on the poster.
The word is **alter**.

Spelling 11: The word is **election**.
They held an **election** to choose the school council.
The word is **election**.

Spelling 12: The word is **discipline**.
Some people consider yoga to be a **discipline** as well as a relaxation method.
The word is **discipline**.

Spelling 13: The word is **decency**.
Her **decency** was obvious when she donated the prize money to the charity.
The word is **decency**.

Spelling 14: The word is **receive**.
He was so proud to **receive** the award for bravery.
The word is **receive**.

Spelling 15: The word is **guessed**.
The children **guessed** their teacher's age accurately.
The word is **guessed**.

Spelling 16: The word is **permission**.
Permission to leave at lunchtime was awarded to the most responsible children.
The word is **permission**.

Spelling 17: The word is **neighbour**.
He checked that his **neighbour** was safe and sound.
The word is **neighbour**.

Spelling 18: The word is **independence**.
As the kitten grew, its **independence** increased.
The word is **independence**.

Spelling 19: The word is **brought**.
His mum **brought** his forgotten trainers to school.
The word is **brought**.

Spelling 20: The word is **advise**.
Experts **advise** all riders to wear cycling helmets.
The word is **advise**.

Well done! Now I will read the sentences again so you can check your spelling.

| Name | Class | Date |

Year 6/P7 Summer Half Term 2 Test A

1. The _____ massage left the sports player ready for her next game.

2. The top _____ commanded perfection in his kitchen.

3. The _____ grass looked realistic.

4. She was _____ upset by the terrible news.

5. She had to _____ that the necklace might be lost forever.

6. The girl overcame her _____ from the audition and went on to be successful.

7. The _____ in London was spread by fleas on rats.

8. His _____ of children improved when he started helping at school.

9. The data was _____ for hours!

10. Please do not _____ the information on the poster.

11. They held an _____ to choose the school council.

12. Some people consider yoga to be a _____ as well as a relaxation method.

13. Her _____ was obvious when she donated the prize money to the charity.

14. He was so proud to _____ the award for bravery.

15. The children _____ their teacher's age accurately.

16. _____ to leave at lunchtime was awarded to the most responsible children.

17. He checked that his _____ was safe and sound.

18. As the kitten grew, its _____ increased.

19. His mum _____ his forgotten trainers to school.

20. Experts _____ all riders to wear cycling helmets.

Total _____ / 20

Year 6/P7 Summer Half Term 2 Test B

Spelling rules and knowledge

- The words in this test can be used to revise content from the spelling rules for Years 3 and 4 and Years 5 and 6.

Guidance for teachers

The test is designed to build experience and confidence with this format, as well as to test children's spelling knowledge.
The test should take approximately 15 minutes.
Children should have a copy of the test and a pencil to use.
Children with specific needs should be given appropriate support.
All children should be encouraged to have a go at spelling each word, using the strategies that they have learnt.
Remind the children to check their answers by asking: *Does it look right? Does it sound right? Does it make sense in the sentence?*
Avoid over-emphasising the spelling of each word as you read it.

> Read each word aloud, saying: *The word is…*
> Next, read the sentence that includes the word.
> Wait for the children to attempt to write the word.
> Re-read the word, saying: *The word is…*

Remind the children to check the word before moving to the next spelling.
At the end of the test, read each sentence again and encourage the children to check back.

Instructions for children

(You may like to read this to the children prior to the test.)

This is a spelling test to check your knowledge of the spelling words we have worked on.
You need a pencil.
Please write your name, class and the date at the top of the test.
I will read a word out loud and then say it again in a sentence.
You should write the word in the gap in the sentence on your test.
I will read it again and give you time to check it.
Don't worry if you are not sure about a spelling. Have a go using the strategies we have learnt.
If you make a mistake, cross out the word and try again.

Words tested (20)

decision, chorus, gracious, reliable, island, curious, brochure, essential, preference, weather, hesitation, prey, obedience, enough, cereal, musician, fascinate, hesitancy, ceiling, morning

Year 6/P7 Summer Half Term 2 Test B

Spelling script

Spelling 1: The word is **decision**.
It wasn't an easy **decision** to make.
The word is **decision**.

Spelling 2: The word is **chorus**.
The children in the **chorus** all wore red T-shirts.
The word is **chorus**.

Spelling 3: The word is **gracious**.
Goodness **gracious** me! Is that the time?
The word is **gracious**.

Spelling 4: The word is **reliable**.
The watch had stopped being **reliable** years ago.
The word is **reliable**.

Spelling 5: The word is **island**.
The **island** was a sanctuary for wild birds and animals.
The word is **island**.

Spelling 6: The word is **curious**.
The **curious** mouse inched towards the mouse trap.
The word is **curious**.

Spelling 7: The word is **brochure**.
The holiday **brochure** was filled with tantalising pictures.
The word is **brochure**.

Spelling 8: The word Is **essential**.
Sugar is an **essential** ingredient in most cake recipes.
The word is **essential**.

Spelling 9: The word is **preference**.
Her **preference** was for pasta, not rice!
The word is **preference**.

Spelling 10: The word is **weather**.
The **weather** in the UK is becoming more extreme due to climate change.
The word is **weather**.

Spelling 11: The word is **hesitation**.
His **hesitation** lost him the match.
The word is **hesitation**.

Spelling 12: The word is **prey**.
An eagle is an awesome bird of **prey**.
The word is **prey**.

Spelling 13: The word is **obedience**.
The **obedience** class was full of naughty puppies!
The word is **obedience**.

Spelling 14: The word is **enough**.
There were **enough** presents for all the children.
The word is **enough**.

Spelling 15: The word is **cereal**.
The hotel breakfast included a wide choice of **cereal** brands.
The word is **cereal**.

Spelling 16: The word is **musician**.
The talented **musician** arrived at the festival carrying his precious guitar.
The word is **musician**.

Spelling 17: The word is **fascinate**.
The magician aimed to **fascinate** his audience with his sleight of hand.
The word is **fascinate**.

Spelling 18: The word is **hesitancy**.
There was no **hesitancy** in her voice as she began to read aloud.
The word is **hesitancy**.

Spelling 19: The word is **ceiling**.
The crack in the **ceiling** grew as the earth shook!
The word is **ceiling**.

Spelling 20: The word is **morning**.
She loved her first cup of tea in the **morning**!
The word is **morning**.

Well done! Now I will read the sentences again so you can check your spelling.

| Name | Class | Date |

Year 6/P7 Summer Half Term 2 Test B

1. It wasn't an easy _____ to make.

2. The children in the _____ all wore red T-shirts.

3. Goodness _____ me! Is that the time?

4. The watch had stopped being _____ years ago.

5. The _____ was a sanctuary for wild birds and animals.

6. The _____ mouse inched towards the mouse trap.

7. The holiday _____ was filled with tantalising pictures.

8. Sugar is an _____ ingredient in most cake recipes.

9. Her _____ was for pasta, not rice!

10. The _____ in the UK is becoming more extreme due to climate change.

11. His _____ lost him the match.

12. An eagle is an awesome bird of _____.

13. The _____ class was full of naughty puppies!

14. There were _____ presents for all the children.

15. The hotel breakfast included a wide choice of _____ brands.

16. The talented _____ arrived at the festival carrying his precious guitar.

17. The magician aimed to _____ his audience with his sleight of hand.

18. There was no _____ in her voice as she began to read aloud.

19. The crack in the _____ grew as the earth shook!

20. She loved her first cup of tea in the _____!

Total _____ / 20

Answers in Context

Year 6/P7 Autumn Half Term 1 Test A

1. We had to **accommodate** the extra guest in the caravan.

2. The boy was **available** to play in the match.

3. The **competition** was tough to play the lead role in the play.

4. She was **determined** to prove her mum wrong.

5. The boy had an **excellent** school report again.

6. She was desperate to **achieve** top marks in the test.

7. Mum found an absolute **bargain** at the market.

8. The penalty that was awarded caused huge **controversy**.

9. The avalanche had **disastrous** consequences for the ski resort.

10. The stranger at the back of the hall looked **familiar**.

Answers in Context

11. She **accidentally** rode into the back of her friend's bike.

12. Sometimes it is hard to **breathe** when you have a cold.

13. Please **complete** the test to the best of your ability.

14. The octopus squeezed each of its **eight** legs into the old jar in the tank.

15. We inched **forward** slowly in the traffic jam.

16. Please **address** the letter in your best handwriting.

17. "It's none of your **business**!" snapped the irritated teacher.

18. Please **decide** who you want to work with today.

19. Press ups are my least favourite **exercise**.

20. The **group** of teenagers played at the skate park.

Answers in Context

Year 6/P7 Autumn Half Term 1 Test B

1. We wanted to **accompany** our guest at all times.

2. The **average** number of hours that people sleep for each night is eight.

3. It was on his **conscience** that he had told a lie.

4. Please can you **develop** your answer further?

5. The **existence** of dinosaurs has been proved by their fossils and skeletons.

6. The **aggressive** hound snarled at the police officer.

7. The **bruise** on my hip stopped me getting to sleep.

8. The **convenience** store sold food and drinks from 7:00 a.m. to 11:00 p.m.

9. "Please try not to **embarrass** me!" the girl said to her mum.

10. We are so excited to be going on a **foreign** holiday.

Answers in Context

11. The **actual** time that the sun rose was 7:00 a.m.

12. Let's **build** a den in the woods.

13. It is important to **consider** your teammates' feelings.

14. Neptune is the **eighth** planet in distance from the sun.

15. The **fruit** bowl contained a pineapple and a mango.

16. He **actually** deserved to win the race, even though he tripped at the last stage.

17. The city gets so **busy** on Saturdays.

18. Please **continue** to read quietly to the end.

19. Are there **enough** chairs for everyone?

20. My dad helps me with my **grammar** homework.

Answers in Context

Year 6/P7 Autumn Half Term 2 Test A

1. It was **apparent** that he was out of breath.

2. The **committee** decided to appoint a new chairperson.

3. His **curiosity** got the better of him!

4. Our camping **equipment** was ready to pack.

5. The **government** changed after the election.

6. I am very **attached** to my family and friends.

7. We are building a new **community** playground for the children.

8. She was **desperate** for a drink after the race.

9. The fisherman liked to **exaggerate** about the size of his catch.

10. It's important not to **harass** a new pet but to let it settle.

Answers in Context

11. If you know the **answer**, please put up your hand.

12. We keep a record of our guitar lessons on the **calendar**.

13. He had to try to **describe** the thief's appearance to the detective.

14. Your first residential trip can be a daunting **experience**.

15. The **guard** dog growled at the intruder.

16. Please **arrive** punctually at 6:00 p.m.

17. The sports **centre** had a new gymnasium.

18. It is **difficult** for some people to stand on their head.

19. The **extreme** weather meant we couldn't leave the house.

20. We **heard** the whistle but carried on playing anyway!

Answers in Context

Year 6/P7 Autumn Half Term 2 Test B

1. The **amateur** boxer dreaded entering the ring.

2. She competed in the swimming gala for her age **category**.

3. We sometimes **correspond** by email; sometimes by letter.

4. We can make our **environment** more pleasant by planting flowers.

5. When Dad was **forty** we had a big party.

6. He didn't **appreciate** the effort they had made.

7. They tried to **communicate** using sign language.

8. He made a **definite** offer in the auction.

9. The apple pie was **especially** sweet.

10. The **guarantee** expired the day before the washing machine broke down.

Answers in Context

11. The birds didn't **appear**, even though we watched all afternoon.

12. She **caught** a cold on her birthday!

13. We go to bed at **different** times in the holidays.

14. The science **experiment** went disastrously wrong.

15. They hired a **guide** to help them tour the famous sites.

16. He couldn't **believe** how much money it cost.

17. We live in the twenty-first **century**.

18. We watched the dolphins **disappear** beneath the waves.

19. The **famous** footballer scored a hat-trick in the first half.

20. Your **heart** pumps blood around your body.

Answers in Context

Year 6/P7 Spring Half Term 1 Test A

1. My little sister was a real **hindrance** on the bike ride.

2. The trip to the film studios was a **marvellous** treat.

3. The girl tried to **persuade** her sister to eat a spider.

4. He made a **relevant** contribution to the discussion.

5. The eager **soldier** volunteered to lead the march.

6. Please respond **immediately** if you hear the siren.

7. It is not **necessary** to wear your hat and scarf today.

8. It has been a **privilege** to be here today.

9. The drummer had an outstanding sense of **rhythm**.

10. I **suggest** you come running tomorrow.

Answers in Context

11. He tried to **imagine** life without ice cream.

12. The **medicine** had the most appalling flavour.

13. It soon became apparent that he was no **ordinary** guitar player.

14. The **pressure** in her bicycle tyres was too low, so she had to pump them up.

15. The man had to serve a 20-year **sentence** in prison.

16. The children had little **interest** in the choice of activities on offer.

17. The Grand Canyon is a **natural** wonder.

18. **Perhaps** you would like to try skating today.

19. She trod on her brother's toe on **purpose**.

20. The boy drew a completely **straight** line with his ruler.

Answers in Context

Year 6/P7 Spring Half Term 1 Test B

1. We competed to work out the **identity** of the murderer in the game.

2. The **mischievous** kitten would not come inside.

3. She had to pass a **physical** test to get into the army.

4. The French **restaurant** served snails in garlic.

5. His **stomach** ache stopped him from running the cross-country course.

6. Each **individual** statue had a different expression.

7. My **neighbour** fed my hamster when I was away.

8. The dentist considered her **profession** to be worthy.

9. The tribespeople might **sacrifice** one of their animals in a ceremony.

10. An emoji is a **symbol** that communicates a message.

Answers in Context

11. We watched the water inside our rowing boat **increase** as we rowed across the lake.

12. He tried not to **mention** the bad news.

13. She was extremely agitated on that **particular** day.

14. I could **probably** make it to the train station on time.

15. Try not to become **separate** from the rest of the group.

16. He carried the **important** letter inside his jacket.

17. In one **minute**, there are sixty seconds.

18. The strange potion made her feel extremely **peculiar**.

19. If I make a **promise**, then I will keep it.

20. My birthday is always a **special** day.

Answers in Context

Year 6/P7 Spring Half Term 2 Test A

1. The stranger was speaking in a foreign **language**.

2. Multiples of 10 **occur** alternately in the 5 times table.

3. We had to **queue** for an ice cream.

4. I have been practising writing my **signature**.

5. The search for the missing socks was very **thorough**.

6. Thunder usually booms a few seconds after **lightning** has flashed.

7. The Houses of **Parliament** are in central London.

8. The librarian could **recommend** great new authors to try.

9. He was **sincerely** sorry for the trouble he caused.

10. There was a great **variety** of vegetables in the market.

Answers in Context

11. The **island** looked beautiful from the plane window.

12. The **naughty** children had to stay in at lunchtime.

13. The most **popular** musician won all the prizes at the ceremony.

14. You can have a snack at **quarter** to eleven.

15. She had a **strange** premonition when she saw the gloomy old house.

16. It is hard to **learn** a new skill when you are tired and hungry!

17. We wore our best clothes for the grand **occasion**.

18. I only **possess** one working handwriting pen!

19. The **recent** film had attracted huge crowds to the cinema.

20. Do you **suppose** that I could have a cup of tea?

Answers in Context

Year 6/P7 Spring Half Term 2 Test B

1. Please do not **interfere** with the computer while it is updating.

2. The wasps were a terrible **nuisance** at the picnic.

3. Her favourite television **programme** was cancelled due to the breaking news.

4. Her **secretary** sent an email to cancel the meeting.

5. The new booking **system** was a huge success.

6. At the **leisure** centre, there are three trampolines.

7. The **opportunity** to hold the python was exciting!

8. He didn't **recognise** his sister after so many years apart.

9. He gave his **sincere** apologies for missing the special dinner party.

10. The **twelfth** month of the year is December.

Answers in Context

11. **Knowledge** may be recorded in encyclopaedias.

12. The **notice** was pinned up where it could not be missed.

13. Her **position** in the league table dropped from second to third.

14. The police officer was ready to **question** the thief.

15. Your **strength** will improve if you lift weights.

16. Each **length** of the swimming pool made his arms more tired.

17. **Occasionally** we are allowed fizzy drinks with dinner.

18. His most precious **possession** was his football shirt.

19. She visited her granny on a **regular** basis.

20. The present was a wonderful **surprise**.

Answers in Context

Year 6/P7 Summer Half Term 1 Test A

1. The rotten **vegetable** made the fridge smell terrible.

2. She had **forgotten** to wear a sun hat again.

3. The boy would often **disagree** with his dad about his bedtime.

4. We waited anxiously for our cat to **reappear**.

5. The **information** was presented in a clear manner.

6. Even **though** she was really hungry, she wouldn't eat the rice.

7. The puppy **preferred** its smelly old blanket to the new cushion.

8. She **misheard** the instructions and arrived ten minutes late.

9. The book's **subtitle** made it sound more interesting.

10. He **usually** carried his own wetsuit to the beach.

Answers in Context

11. He tried to squeeze **through** the hole in the fence.

12. The famous **mystery** was a legend in their town.

13. It is **illegal** to drive without a seatbelt.

14. At the **international** tournament, players from every continent took part.

15. The tailor took care to **measure** the client precisely.

16. The **woman** in the interview made a convincing argument for healthy eating.

17. I thought I was seeing **double** when I looked at the twins!

18. Our report must not contain **irrelevant** information.

19. Their promotion was **automatic** because they won the league.

20. The **teacher** asked the children to work in pairs.

Answers in Context

Year 6/P7 Summer Half Term 1 Test B

1. Will the owner of the red **vehicle** please move it away from the entrance?

2. At the **beginning**, there was an eerie silence.

3. The **dishonest** tradesman was caught red-handed.

4. I want to **rearrange** my bedroom furniture to make more space.

5. Flying through the air is a strange **sensation**.

6. **Although** she was eager, she waited until last.

7. The **gardening** chores were never-ending!

8. She had real **misfortune** when she lost her phone and bag on the same day.

9. Some weightlifters appear to have **superhuman** strength.

10. **Originally**, we were aiming to arrive at 1:00 p.m.

Answers in Context

11. Of all the **various** birds in the garden, the goldfinch is my favourite.

12. He had my **sympathy** when he broke his finger.

13. Learning to ski seemed like an **impossible** challenge.

14. Dad put **antiseptic** on my wound.

15. The holiday promised to be a great **adventure**.

16. The baby elephant's **weight** had nearly doubled!

17. You have to **touch** your ticket on the reader to open the barrier.

18. His **irresponsible** actions led to him being grounded!

19. She treasured the actor's **autograph** forever.

20. Behind the **picture** there was a locked safe.

Answers in Context

Year 6/P7 Summer Half Term 2 Test A

1. The **vigorous** massage left the sports player ready for her next game.

2. The top **chef** commanded perfection in his kitchen.

3. The **artificial** grass looked realistic.

4. She was **visibly** upset by the terrible news.

5. She had to **accept** that the necklace might be lost forever.

6. The girl overcame her **rejection** from the audition and went on to be successful.

7. The **plague** in London was spread by fleas on rats.

8. His **tolerance** of children improved when he started helping at school.

9. The data was **transferring** for hours!

10. Please do not **alter** the information on the poster.

Answers in Context

11. They held an **election** to choose the school council.

12. Some people consider yoga to be a **discipline** as well as a relaxation method.

13. Her **decency** was obvious when she donated the prize money to the charity.

14. He was so proud to **receive** the award for bravery.

15. The children **guessed** their teacher's age accurately.

16. **Permission** to leave at lunchtime was awarded to the most responsible children.

17. He checked that his **neighbour** was safe and sound.

18. As the kitten grew, its **independence** increased.

19. His mum **brought** his forgotten trainers to school.

20. Experts **advise** all riders to wear cycling helmets.

Answers in Context

Year 6/P7 Summer Half Term 2 Test B

1. It wasn't an easy **decision** to make.

2. The children in the **chorus** all wore red T-shirts.

3. Goodness **gracious** me! Is that the time?

4. The watch had stopped being **reliable** years ago.

5. The **island** was a sanctuary for wild birds and animals.

6. The **curious** mouse inched towards the mouse trap.

7. The holiday **brochure** was filled with tantalising pictures.

8. Sugar is an **essential** ingredient in most cake recipes.

9. Her **preference** was for pasta, not rice!

10. The **weather** in the UK is becoming more extreme due to climate change.

Answers in Context

11. His **hesitation** lost him the match.

12. An eagle is an awesome bird of **prey**.

13. The **obedience** class was full of naughty puppies!

14. There were **enough** presents for all the children.

15. The hotel breakfast included a wide choice of **cereal** brands.

16. The talented **musician** arrived at the festival carrying his precious guitar.

17. The magician aimed to **fascinate** his audience with his sleight of hand.

18. There was no **hesitancy** in her voice as she began to read aloud.

19. The crack in the **ceiling** grew as the earth shook!

20. She loved her first cup of tea in the **morning**!

Word-only Answers

Year 6/P7 Autumn Half Term 1 Test A
1. accommodate, 2. available, 3. competition,
4. determined, 5. excellent, 6. achieve,
7. bargain, 8. controversy, 9. disastrous,
10. familiar, 11. accidentally, 12. breathe,
13. complete, 14. eight, 15. forward, 16. address, 17. business, 18. decide, 19. exercise, 20. group

Year 6/P7 Autumn Half Term 1 Test B
1. accompany, 2. average, 3. conscience,
4. develop, 5. existence, 6. aggressive, 7. bruise, 8. convenience, 9. embarrass, 10. foreign,
11. actual, 12. build, 13. consider, 14. eighth, 15. fruit, 16. actually, 17. busy, 18. continue, 19. enough, 20. grammar

Year 6/P7 Autumn Half Term 2 Test A
1. apparent, 2. committee, 3. curiosity,
4. equipment, 5. government, 6. attached,
7. community, 8. desperate, 9. exaggerate,
10. harass, 11. answer, 12. calendar,
13. describe, 14. experience, 15. guard,
16. arrive, 17. centre, 18. difficult, 19. extreme, 20. heard

Year 6/P7 Autumn Half Term 2 Test B
1. amateur, 2. category, 3. correspond,
4. environment, 5. forty, 6. appreciate,
7. communicate, 8. definite, 9. especially,
10. guarantee, 11. appear, 12. caught,
13. different, 14. experiment, 15. guide,
16. believe, 17. century, 18. disappear,
19. famous, 20. heart

Year 6/P7 Spring Half Term 1 Test A
1. hindrance, 2. marvellous, 3. persuade,
4. relevant, 5. soldier, 6. immediately,
7. necessary, 8. privilege, 9. rhythm, 10. suggest, 11. imagine, 12. medicine, 13. ordinary,
14. pressure, 15. sentence, 16. interest,
17. natural, 18. perhaps, 19. purpose,
20. straight

Year 6/P7 Spring Half Term 1 Test B
1. identity, 2. mischievous, 3. physical,
4. restaurant, 5. stomach, 6. individual,
7. neighbour, 8. profession, 9. sacrifice,
10. symbol, 11. increase, 12. mention,
13. particular, 14. probably, 15. separate,
16. important, 17. minute, 18. peculiar,
19. promise, 20. special

Year 6/P7 Spring Half Term 2 Test A
1. language, 2. occur, 3. queue, 4. signature,
5. thorough, 6. lightning, 7. parliament,
8. recommend, 9. sincerely, 10. variety,
11. island, 12. naughty, 13. popular, 14. quarter, 15. strange, 16. learn, 17. occasion,
18. possess, 19. recent, 20. suppose

Year 6/P7 Spring Half Term 2 Test B
1. interfere, 2. nuisance, 3. programme,
4. secretary, 5. system, 6. leisure, 7. opportunity, 8. recognise, 9. sincere, 10. twelfth,
11. knowledge, 12. notice, 13. position,
14. question, 15. strength, 16. length,
17. occasionally, 18. possession, 19. regular,
20. surprise

Word-only Answers

Year 6/P7 Summer Half Term 1 Test A
1. vegetable, 2. forgotten, 3. disagree,
4. reappear, 5. information, 6. though,
7. preferred, 8. misheard, 9. subtitle, 10. usually, 11. through, 12. mystery, 13. illegal,
14. international, 15. measure, 16. woman,
17. double, 18. irrelevant, 19. automatic,
20. teacher

Year 6/P7 Summer Half Term 1 Test B
1. vehicle, 2. beginning, 3. dishonest,
4. rearrange, 5. sensation, 6. although,
7. gardening, 8. misfortune, 9. superhuman,
10. originally, 11. various, 12. sympathy,
13. impossible, 14. antiseptic, 15. adventure,
16. weight, 17. touch, 18. irresponsible,
19. autograph, 20. picture

Year 6/P7 Summer Half Term 2 Test A
1. vigorous, 2. chef, 3. artificial, 4. visibly,
5. accept, 6. rejection, 7. plague, 8. tolerance,
9. transferring, 10. alter, 11. election,
12. discipline, 13. decency, 14. receive,
15. guessed, 16. permission, 17. neighbour,
18. independence, 19. brought, 20. advise

Year 6/P7 Summer Half Term 2 Test B
1. decision, 2. chorus, 3. gracious, 4. reliable,
5. island, 6. curious, 7. brochure, 8. essential,
9. preference, 10. weather, 11. hesitation,
12. prey, 13. obedience, 14. enough, 15. cereal,
16. musician, 17. fascinate, 18. hesitancy,
19. ceiling, 20. morning

| Name | Class |

Year 6/P7 Spelling Record Sheet

Tests	Mark	Total marks	Key words to target
Autumn Half Term 1 Test A		20	
Autumn Half Term 1 Test B		20	
Autumn Half Term 2 Test A		20	
Autumn Half Term 2 Test B		20	
Spring Half Term 1 Test A		20	
Spring Half Term 1 Test B		20	
Spring Half Term 2 Test A		20	
Spring Half Term 2 Test B		20	
Summer Half Term 1 Test A		20	
Summer Half Term 1 Test B		20	
Summer Half Term 2 Test A		20	
Summer Half Term 2 Test B		20	

© HarperCollins*Publishers* Ltd 2018

www.ingramcontent.com/pod-product-compliance
Lightning Source LLC
Chambersburg PA
CBHW081419300426
44109CB00019BA/2348